Praise for **Little Erik**

"Jackson, always a theatrical adventurer, smacks all the cobwebs out of Ibsen's text with a vividly contemporary take on the fractured family drama… Jackson's adaptation astutely sharpens the edge of the play… There is no denying that you walk away from the theatre wrestling with the issues that shape all of our lives."

– SAN JOSE MERCURY NEWS

"Jackson brings forth the central issues of Ibsen's original with keen psychological insight. Marriage and mortality, ambition and narcissism, incest, parenthood and social responsibility swirl through this heady, intensely focused production…"

– SAN FRANCISCO EXAMINER

"Taut and at times brutally frank… It plays out in a mix of realism, mysticism and caricature, and of dramatic tension and social satire that varies from engrossing to confounding. …A richly nuanced and uncomfortable study in class prejudice and injustice… [Jackson has] raised the bar in terms of Freddie and Andi's mutual attraction, to riveting effect."

– SAN FRANCISCO CHRONICLE

"Jackson forces us to take account of how we misperceive the world. The symbolic elements of *Little Erik* aren't there as an aesthetic, but rather as a strategy to a more forceful realism and accounting of the world."

– KQED.ORG

"[*Little Erik*] tackles a slew of weighty themes, from guilt to technological dependence… The most inventive strength of Jackson's *Little Erik* lies not in its commentary about anger or betrayal, of which there is plenty. Rather, it's in the production's ability to convincingly characterize a Bay Area fueled by a dependency on technology."

– EAST BAY EXPRESS

"A sound of river currents crash in the background as a woman looks chillingly beyond the audience, into the distance; this is how writer and director Mark Jackson's *Little Erik* begins its 80-minute run. It is the stillness of moments like these that are filled with a dramatic musical hum that gives the entire play a memorable hypnotic power… The issues that the play deals with are timely and reasons alone to watch the play."

– THE DAILY CALIFORNIAN

Mark Jackson

LITTLE ERIK

EXIT
PRESS

Little Erik
by Mark Jackson
Copyright © 2017 by Mark Jackson
All rights reserved

Published by EXIT Press
First Edition: March 2017

Cover design by Kevin Clarke.
Book design by Richard Livingston.
Front cover photo by David Allen, used with permission, from the 2016
Aurora Theatre Company world premiere production of *Little Erik*. Back to
front: Wilma Bonet (rear), Joe Estlack (L) and Mariah Castle (R). See more
of David Allen's photography at www.davidallenstudio.com

For additional information about U.S. copyright laws, go to:
www.copyright.gov

For additional information about Mark Jackson go to:
www.markjackson-theatermaker.com

ISBN: 978-1-941704-13-4

EXIT Press
156 Eddy Street
San Francisco, CA 94102-2708

www.exittheatre.org

Contents

Foreword by Mariah Castle   vii

Little Erik   1

Afterword by Mark Jackson   87

About the author   89

Foreword

Little Erik is not an easy play. It's alive and loaded, messy and electric. It's not the kind of piece that invites you to sit back and enjoy; it's the kind of theatre that challenges you to lean in and engage. At first, I resisted the challenge. Back in 2014, Mark Jackson invited me to read an early draft of his contemporary adaptation of Henrik Ibsen's *Little Eyolf*. By the end of the play my body was curled up in a tense ball at the corner of my couch, my brow furrowed, my heart pounding. I was enlivened but very agitated.

That Mark's work had inspired a visceral reaction in me was nothing new. One of the first productions of his that I saw was *God's Plot* in 2011. I found myself edging my seat, slack-jawed and weeping throughout. I left that show determined to see more of his work. In the years since, his plays have provoked, inspired, shaken, and surprised me.

Mark's work aims to raise the body temperature of everyone in the room. As he told me recently, he believes in the value of contention as a creative force. By forging charged situations onstage, he aims to ignite dialogue and transformation in both the performers and the audience. The character of Joie in *Little Erik*, for example, inspired contentious debate during the play's initial run. Joie, played with searing precision and magnetic power by Marilee Talkington, offered a hard, fiery, unapologetic portrayal of womanhood that was triggering to many. At one point in the script she confesses to her husband, "You know I never wanted a child. But I kept him. For you! Sometimes I hate you for it." Some audience members (and reviewers) were unsettled by her ambivalence about motherhood, her strong sexual appetite, and her unapologetic ambition, while others were greatly relieved by her frankness and ability to articulate experiences that many women have but are afraid to speak about. The characters in *Little Erik* may not be particularly likable but they are relatable—they reflect messy truths that are hard to sit with. Mark celebrates this tension between likeability and relatability by embracing it as an opportunity for growth. As he once said in an interview with the *San Francisco Chronicle*, "For me, it's exciting to do a piece that's about having compassion for people in very emotionally difficult situations when they're not at their best."[1] If we can find empathy for Joie in her darkest hour, perhaps we can be gentler with ourselves.

Part of my initial resistance to the play stemmed from my discomfort with the themes I saw reflected in my own life. But my objections went deeper. When I first read *Little Erik*, I was troubled by the gender archetypes that I saw: the hardened, unfulfilled career woman (Joie), the self-sacrificing caretaker (Andi), and the perpetual man-child (Freddie), each of them seeking, but failing, to connect with one another. As an avowed feminist, I am wary of the limited options that patriarchal cultures prescribe to men and women about who and what they can be. I am also wary of tragic love stories that often result from these prescriptions. No one whose humanity is stifled can fully love. I long to see boundary-pushing narratives in theatre where characters are courageous enough to speak the truth and resist the cultural pressure to quiet their hearts. I didn't see this in *Little Erik*. At least, not at first. Six months after my initial reading, however, I was offered the role of Andi in the world premiere at the Aurora Theatre Company in Berkeley, California. I revisited the text. Over the course of my work on this project, as I mapped out Andi's emotional arc, I uncovered a new narrative that I hadn't seen before.

At the beginning of the play Andi is vibrating with a newly discovered truth that she is both eager and terrified to share with her half-brother, Freddie. This secret reflects a knowing she has carried in her body since she was a teenager. Andi has been playing the "good girl" most of her life, following the rules and sacrificing her own desires to be in service to others. She is now aware that if she releases this secret her core relationships will be irrevocably altered. Rather than choosing the safe, uncontentious route, Andi breaks her silence and reveals the truth to Freddie. The result is chaos. But there is also freedom: Andi recovers her sanity, reclaims her Voice, and liberates herself and Freddie from deep entanglement. Most importantly, Andi becomes an agent of her own desires. She is able to take a leap towards a future that,

---

1 Hamlin, Jesse. "S.F. theatre artist updates Ibsen for our times". *SF Gate* 2016. Web. 22 Oct. 2016.

while still unknown, belongs fully to her. We realize, by the end, that this is a story built around Andi's journey. Even the title reflects her name. Little Erik is the name of Freddie and Joie's son (whose tragic death spurs much of the dramatic action of the play) but it is also Freddie's childhood nickname for Andi. We've been speaking her name all along without realizing it.

The journey that *Little Erik* offers may not be easy but it is one that I embrace. It is bumpy but revealing. While it reflects some uncomfortably honest and familiar archetypes, it also subverts gender expectations and reveals itself to be a story of reclamation and hope. Andi's journey to find her voice and speak the truth was an inspiring one for me to embody as a performer. I'm grateful that I did not abandon this play when I found it unsettling and challenging. By questioning my discomfort and engaging in a dialogue around the work, I uncovered a deeper degree of compassion for myself and others and an inspiring narrative of truth-seeking. I hope you will too.

Mariah Castle
February 2017

Little Erik

Little Erik was first produced by Aurora Theatre Company, Berkeley, CA. Tom Ross, Artistic Director. Julie Saltzman, Managing Director. The world premiere was held there on February 4, 2016. The production was directed by the author, with the following cast and staff:

JOIE	Marilee Talkington
ANDI	Mariah Castle
FREDDIE	Joe Estlack
ERIK	Jack Wittmayer
THE RAT WIFE	Wilma Bonet
BERNIE	Greg Ayers
Scenery	Nina Ball
Costumes	Christine Crook
Lights	Heather Basarab
Sound	Matt Stines
Video	Wolfgang Wachalovsky
Stage Manager	Susan Reamy

Characters

Joie, makes bank in the tech industry.
Freddie, her husband.
Erik, their disabled nine-year-old son.
Andi, a high school English teacher and Freddie's slightly younger half-sister.
Bernie, an architect.
The Rat Wife, an itinerant worker (she says).

Time & Place

Today. Toward the end of a record hot summer also notable for its occasional off-season snow flurries. In a lovely area near a river just north of San Francisco. The kind of place where people of means have expensively minimalist summer or second homes.

Notes

Little Erik *is oh so freely adapted from the basic scenario of Henrik Ibsen's* Little Eyolf.

Although what's on the page might suggest some variant of a strictly realistic design and performance approach, a production should not go unquestioningly along with that obvious suggestion. The dialogue is basically "realistic," yet there is a strange interaction between nature and human emotion. And of course a RAT WIFE appears and drowns a child under mysterious circumstances. An approach that allows the event to be theatre, in other words metaphor, would be appropriate. Likewise, it is useful to consider that comedy and tragedy are shadows of one another, and the truth is always both funny and tragic.

The ethnic possibilities of characters should be considered during casting. For example, it could be interesting if BERNIE, who has never been to India, is Indian-American. Or if a Japanese-American actor is found who's great for that role, BERNIE's destination could be changed to Japan.

Similarly, the spelling of JOIE's name comes from a Chinese friend of mine, and I'd thought of JOIE as being Chinese-American. She could also be of some other heritage. Choices in casting will bring out various dramatic complications around the class issues at work in the play, and productions should consider what would be most productively provocative in their context.

Choices in this regard should impact decisions made around lines in [brackets], and whether they are kept, cut, or altered. [There are a few other alternate lines in brackets related to matters other than race that productions may consider.]

The last thing on this theme I'll add is a request that productions be truthful in their choices, not politically correct. I've hoped to write a play about complicated people, and such people seldom make good poster children for any point of view.

A slash (/) at the top of a line means it overlaps at a logical point in the previous line. A dash (–) at the top of a line means one should come in tightly to the previous line. A dash (–) at the end of a line means a thought is being cut off, either by the speaker or the next character to speak. Actors should consider all punctuation, capitalization, as well as stage directions, alongside the words.

Scene One

As the audience enters it is snowing on stage. When the performance begins, a mighty wind blows all the snow away and a hot summer sun comes out.

In the house. Late morning. JOIE is alone. ANDI arrives. There is already an ambiguous tension in the air. Like a Hitchcock film.

JOIE

Andi.

ANDI

Oh.

JOIE

What are you doing here?

ANDI

What?

JOIE

I thought you were done coming up here.

ANDI

I was.

JOIE

You're back.

ANDI

I'm sorry, I didn't know you'd be here. …I've gotten so used to coming and going. You've been very generous. I appreciate it. … It's so beautiful here. It's made settling Dad's business easier to take, being able to get away so often, and spending time here with Erik. So, thank you. …I can go, it's no problem.

JOIE

You're here now. Sit down.

ANDI

Thank you.

JOIE

Stop thanking me. You broke the place in for us. Took Erik up here all those weekends. Dealt with Bernie. Everything looks great. I don't know where anything is, but Erik seems to know his way around. Last night was the first I've spent here, actually. I can tell it's going to take some getting used to. Spotty connection and all.

ANDI

I hadn't planned to come up this weekend. …I've been feeling uneasy in the city. The whole city has felt strange the past few days. That odd weather. And now it's so hot again. And today the air was so still and… strange… Have you had that feeling?

JOIE

Not about the city, no. The snow was strange. Who was it said the coldest summer he ever spent was in San Francisco?

ANDI

Mark Twain.

JOIE

–And that was a long time ago. So it's not THAT strange. The weather.

ANDI

–It's not just the weather.

A silence. JOIE takes a sip of whatever she's drinking.

ANDI *(cont'd)*

Whcre IS Erik?

JOIE

With Freddie.

ANDI

What? Freddie? Is Freddie back?

JOIE

Thursday.

ANDI

Really! He didn't tell me he was coming back!

JOIE

He didn't tell me either. But there he was when I got home from work.

ANDI

Oh. Where is he? I'm sorry, you're here for a family weekend. I should go. I'd love to see him though.

JOIE

Of course. I'm sure they'll be back soon.

ANDI

I wonder if that's what I've been feeling then.

JOIE

What.

ANDI

Freddie's return.

JOIE

I doubt the weather has anything to do with Freddie. He's not THAT important.

ANDI

That's just like him. Freddie does what he wants.

JOIE

Like the weather.

ANDI

I hadn't heard from him in a while.

JOIE

Oh good I'm glad it wasn't just me.

ANDI

He hadn't been posting any updates, nothing. I was starting to worry.

JOIE

I'd think you'd be more used to it than me. You've known him the longest.

ANDI

I've never gotten used to Freddie's silences. But I suppose they make it more fun when he suddenly turns up.

JOIE

Fun. Yes. I remember that about him. You have more patience for his whims than I do. Well, and of course he and I are married and not brother and sister. So it's different.

ANDI

Of course.

JOIE

–When it's your husband that's away for half a year and not IMing or Skyping or posting.

ANDI

–Of course.

JOIE

–Or anything.

ANDI

…When was the last time YOU'D heard from him.

JOIE

Two weeks ago.

ANDI

Two weeks.

JOIE

–And given nearly all my waking hours I'm connected, the silence was really loud.

ANDI

Just don't check your phone so often.

JOIE

Don't what?

ANDI

Don't check your phone so often.

JOIE

I'm sorry. You must be speaking a foreign language.

ANDI

I said don't check your phone–

JOIE

/ I understood what you said, Andi. It's just that it's an absurd thing to say to me. My entire business—this house—is predicated on my checking my phone, often.

ANDI

Right.

JOIE

–The company wouldn't now own a fifth of San Francisco if I wasn't checking my phone often.

ANDI

Right.

JOIE

…Sorry. You're not the only one with a strange feeling.

JOIE takes a sip of her drink.

ANDI

…Is Freddie all right?

JOIE

–Freddie? Beaming.

ANDI

Oh. Did he finish his book then?

JOIE

No.

ANDI

Oh. Then what's he beaming about. He went on this trip—well, because of our father passing. But also to finish his book.

JOIE

That's what he said when he left, yes. You know Freddie. He went looking like he might murder himself and came back fit and tan and beaming like the fucking sunshine. Until we put Erik to bed. Then he crashed like the Hindenburg. We haven't even had a chance to talk yet really.

ANDI

I'm sure he's exhausted from the jet lag. Anyway it sounds like the trip worked.

JOIE

Hopefully. I don't mean to sound negative. Do I sound "negative"? I love him. It's hard to be apart for so long. I don't know how HE did it. Bastard. Pisses me off actually. How hard is it to fire off an Instagram or Facebook post? I can do a dozen of each in a minute plus an email or two to any Luddites.

ANDI

Not all of us are as wired as you, Joie. Freddie and I have never been–

JOIE

/ I know I know. You're artists.

ANDI

Well not me.

JOIE

English teacher? Same thing.

ANDI

Not quite.

JOIE

Words by dead guys.

ANDI

I teach those, yes. Freddie writes his own.

JOIE

You mean his novel? Or his poems! Even worse! Nobody reads
poems. Do your—what are they? Inner city youth? Do they actually
read those old books you assign them?

ANDI

Yes they do.

JOIE

Really? You don't think they just Google a synopsis? …Of course
nobody's ever gonna Google Freddie's synopsis, much less read it.
Because he's never going to write it.

ANDI

Joie!

JOIE

I expected him to finally plunk that novel down in front of me
when he came back. On actual paper, knowing him; he's so
romantic that way. Finished, in any case. That Was the Goal.

ANDI

He's not goal oriented.

JOIE

No kidding. It was HIS epiphany that we build this house you may recall. He fussed over all the plans with Bernie. Then no sooner has the first tree been cut but Freddie is off on a sojourn. He dropped one whim for another. Lucky he had you to stand in for him with Bernie.

ANDI

How was he to know our father would die. He needed some time.

JOIE

What about you, don't you need time? I think Freddie took advantage of you.

ANDI

No, I wanted to handle our Dad's business. It's better that I have something to do.

JOIE

Sure.

ANDI

And I've enjoyed looking after the house… Anyway Freddie's back and feeling better and that's great.

JOIE

It is. Oh: Bernie stopped by yesterday looking for you.

ANDI

Oh.

JOIE

–But I told him you were done coming out here.

ANDI

That's just as well.

JOIE

Don't you like Bernie?

ANDI

He's very nice.

JOIE

Gotcha.

ANDI

I don't mean nice in a bad way.

JOIE

Everyone knows high school English teachers like the bad boys. Heathcliff? Oh right, that's just fantasy. –Excuse me: fiction. Maybe I should read some old books. I'm tired of HBO and Internet porn.

ANDI

You do not look at Internet porn.

JOIE

Don't say you don't.

ANDI

That's for men.

JOIE

Except the porn that's made for women. Get on that, Andi.

ANDI laughs slightly uncomfortably.

JOIE (*cont'd*)

Freddie and I haven't been apart this long before and I'm not used to it. Our bed feels big and empty. I light candles for atmosphere and it's like a funeral parlor. My limbs ache. I can take care of myself of course but it's not the same. My body misses him. …You know I left a man who called me darling when he made love to me for Freddie who called me slut when he fucked me. …Sorry.

ANDI

No no.

JOIE

–I'm sure you can understand.

ANDI

–No yes no no yeah.

A silence.

JOIE

Well, WE just failed the Bechdel Test miserably, didn't we.

ANDI

Where ARE the boys anyway?

JOIE

They jumped up early and went out, probably down to that river again.

ANDI

He can't be that tired, then.

JOIE

Doesn't take much to keep up with Erik.

JOIE takes one step with an affected limp as she starts off across the room.

ANDI

(*chuckling despite herself*) Joie, that's terrible.

JOIE

Oh come on. Cripple jokes are funny. And he's my son so I can joke about it. Probably they're reading together. Freddie has always been determined to make a little professor out of him.

ANDI

He does keep Erik on a regimen.

JOIE

Yeah, but Erik's a kid of his time and I'm pretty sure he'll stay on my side.

ANDI

Your side?

JOIE

The digital side. You know, the future? By which I mean the present. Erik changes by the second. LIKE Freddie I suppose, only not analog.

FREDDIE and ERIK enter, ERIK on FREDDIE'S back. ERIK has an expensive crutch attached to his arm and/or brace to his leg. He dresses a bit fabulously for his age. FREDDIE drops ERIK to greet his sister.

FREDDIE

Andi!

ERIK

/ Aunt Andi!

ANDI

Freddie! Why didn't you tell anyone you were coming back?

FREDDIE

A spur of the moment decision.

ANDI

Okay, but do they communicate by foot messenger over there? Phone break? Internet cafe? Hi Erik.

ANDI hugs ERIK, who is already hugging her enthusiastically.

ERIK

Hi!

FREDDIE

Actually I've sworn off technology.

JOIE

What?

FREDDIE

Yep.

JOIE

Like, forever?

FREDDIE

Probably not. But I'm trying it out.

JOIE

How's that going to work?

FREDDIE

–How is it you happen to be here?

ANDI

Spur of the moment decision. I didn't think anyone would be here, least of all you. You DO look great.

FREDDIE

I feel great.

ANDI

Although I hear you didn't finish your book.

FREDDIE

Didn't touch it.

ANDI

Didn't touch it!

FREDDIE

Not one line.

ANDI

Why? That's why you went.

FREDDIE

Well–

ANDI

–And Dad.

FREDDIE

It's a long story.

JOIE

Six months.

FREDDIE

But it's a good one.

ANDI

What did you do, what happened?

FREDDIE

I thought a lot.

JOIE

About?

FREDDIE

You.

JOIE

Liar.

ANDI

But not about your novel. How are you so happy? It tears you up when you have trouble writing.

FREDDIE

I had no trouble writing. I didn't write. I DID things. In oceans. In mountain lakes. In forests. In places so ancient you can actually see what matters. Wherever I went I got straight out of the city. And at one point, while watching a ridiculous Corsican sunset, it dawned on me what an idiot I've been all my life. Writing? "Ha Ha!" Action! It's doing a thing that matters. Writing it down is pointless.

ANDI

What?

JOIE

He's exaggerating.

FREDDIE

I am absolutely serious. I renounce writing. Plenty of other people
are writing. Way too many. From now on I'm going to live by deeds,
the path less chosen. It's ancient wisdom; if everyone would do
it the world would be a much better place. And more articulate.
Words mean nothing.

JOIE

That is absurdly simplistic.

FREDDIE

–At their best, in the end, words mean very little.

ERIK

Dad, you're really not going to write your book?

FREDDIE

No sir.

ERIK

Then I'll never get to read it.

FREDDIE

You can imagine it.

ANDI

What are you going to do instead?

FREDDIE

Climb mountains as often as I can.

JOIE

Hold on.

ERIK

Can I go with you?

FREDDIE

Of course. Someday.

ERIK does a little hip hop dance move awkwardly and almost falls over.

FREDDIE (*cont'd*)

Woah! Be careful.

ERIK

Aunt Andi do you like my *ensémble*?

ANDI

Yes.

ERIK

I wore it in honor of Dad coming back.

JOIE

Don't be too flattered. Any excuse to wear it will do. It's just about all he'll wear lately.

FREDDIE

Really? You let him out like that?

JOIE

Let him out? Like a dog?

FREDDIE

No.

ERIK starts barking like a dog while working his outfit.

JOIE

It's fine, he likes it, who cares. Besides if I say no he goes diva on me. Don'cha.

ERIK

Can we go swimming?

FREDDIE

Swimming? Is he swimming?

JOIE

He wants to learn how to swim.

FREDDIE

You want to learn how to swim?

ERIK

I want to be a professional swimmer.

ANDI

He saw the other kids swimming in the river.

ERIK

And then you know what I want to be after that?

FREDDIE

What?

ERIK

A rapper.

FREDDIE

A rapper?

ERIK busts out his dance again, this time without falling.

FREDDIE (*cont'd*)

What has happened?

JOIE

If you had been in contact more often you'd be up on these things.

FREDDIE

You want to be a swimming rapper?

ERIK

No! A swimmer. Then a rapper. When can we go to the river? Maybe we'll see the rat wife.

FREDDIE

Is she still around?

ANDI

I just saw her, walking up the main road on the drive up.

JOIE

She was standing by the turnoff yesterday, didn't you see her staring at us?

ERIK

Why is she called the rat wife.

ANDI

That's just what people around here call her. Her real name is Loba.

JOIE

You talked to her?

ANDI

Once, down by the river.

ERIK

What does Loba mean?

ANDI

Wolf in Spanish.

ERIK

Why isn't she called the Wolf Wife.

ANDI

I don't know. She's a cleaning woman, she said, and apparently especially good at getting rid of pests, like rats.

JOIE

Are there rats in this house?

ANDI

No.

FREDDIE

–Erik, why don't you go down to the river now and I'll catch up with you.

ERIK

You come with me.

FREDDIE

I'm gonna talk to your mom and Aunt Andi for a bit.

ERIK

I don't want to go alone.

FREDDIE

You can do it. Just go slowly. And take your phone.

ERIK

Nooooo.

ANDI

He doesn't like to go alone. The other boys.

FREDDIE

What about them?

JOIE

Some urchins made fun of him.

ANDI

He didn't know what they meant.

JOIE

He can tell.

FREDDIE

Did he go to the river dressed like that?

ANDI

Something like that.

FREDDIE

Well.

ANDI

And he told them he wanted to be a rapper.

ERIK

They make fun of me.

JOIE

They're jealous.

FREDDIE

Of what?

JOIE

They're barefoot poor kids. And Erik's clearly not.

FREDDIE

I don't want other kids making fun of him.

ERIK

Then come with me.

FREDDIE

We'll go later, when nobody's there. Whose kids are they, do we know?

ANDI

They're always there, I don't know who they belong to.

THE RAT WIFE appears. Her presence seems to alter time and space. Only ERIK sees her at first.

ERIK

The rat wife's here.

The ADULTS turn and see THE RAT WIFE and are vocally surprised.

THE RAT WIFE

Sorry. Do you need help here?

JOIE

I don't think so, thank you.

THE RAT WIFE

Anything gnawing at your house?

JOIE

No.

THE RAT WIFE

I can help you with that.

FREDDIE

Thank you, but we don't need help. Sorry.

THE RAT WIFE

Oh... I saw that you came. The whole family. I thought I would offer my help, if you need it.

JOIE

We don't, thank you.

THE RAT WIFE

Oh... I'm so tired. It's a steep climb to here.

FREDDIE

You can sit down for a moment if you need to.

JOIE

Freddie.

FREDDIE

–Outside. There's a patio there. You probably saw it. You're welcome to rest there for a minute.

THE RAT WIFE

/ Such a beautiful house. A nice place for a family.

JOIE

Just on weekends now and then. We won't be here much so we won't need help cleaning. But thank you.

THE RAT WIFE

Oh… I'm so tired.

FREDDIE

As I said please feel free to sit down and rest.

THE RAT WIFE does. But inside.

THE RAT WIFE

Gracias. I've been hard at work. I work for many people. Too many people.

ANDI

Me recuerdas? Nos conocimos en el río.

THE RAT WIFE

Sí. Recuerdo. (*to ERIK*) AND I remember you. (*to JOIE and FREDDIE*) And I've been waiting for you.

JOIE

Andi is my husband's sister. She'll also be here from time to time. So we won't need any help.

THE RAT WIFE

Oh… I work for many people. (*laughs*) They don't like the work I do at first. But then they see. Sometimes you have to bite the sour apple. The sour apple, little señor, the sour apple.

ERIK

Who would?

THE RAT WIFE

Qué.

ERIK

Who would eat a sour apple?

THE RAT WIFE

People who have a house full of rats and rat babies.

JOIE

We don't have rats. So we won't need your services. Freddie.

THE RAT WIFE

The little rats by the river, they laughed at your clothes. You remember?

JOIE

Freddie.

FREDDIE

How are you feeling now, better?

THE RAT WIFE

There are rats everywhere. And so many kinds. Old rats. Young. Poor rats. Fat rats. Angry rats. Even happy rats; they don't even know they're a rat. Some are so loud. Some are so quiet you don't even notice they are there. But a rat is always hungry. Always they are wanting something more. If you don't– tratar con ellos…?

ANDI

Uh. Deal with them.

THE RAT WIFE

Deal with them, they find a way. They are very clever. I know what they want. That's why they follow me. Sweet animals. They make me so tired. It's so hard to take care of them.

ERIK

How do you get them to follow you?

THE RAT WIFE looks at ERIK a moment, then pulls out some kind of wooden wind instrument and plays a slow, enticing tune on it. Or maybe she hands it to ERIK to touch and we just hear it. In any case, it's genuinely alluring, and when it's done nobody has moved.

ERIK (*cont'd*)

What do you do with them?

THE RAT WIFE

We go for a swim. All the way down the river to the sea.

ERIK

Rats swim?

JOIE

No. Rats hate water. I read that.

THE RAT WIFE

Yes. But that's why they come with me. They're afraid. And I give them fuerza, coraje.

ERIK

What?

ANDI

Strength and courage.

THE RAT WIFE

They're grateful to me.

ERIK

Don't they drown?

THE RAT WIFE

Every last one.

JOIE

Freddie, please.

FREDDIE

–Okay. You're feeling better?

THE RAT WIFE

Down there it's all as still and soft and dark as their little hearts can desire. Down there they sleep a long, sweet sleep, with no more pain and no one to hate them or to torment them anymore. There was a time, a long time ago, I lured more than rats.

ERIK

What.

THE RAT WIFE

People. One most of all.

ERIK

Who?

THE RAT WIFE

My sweetheart. Oh he was a heart breaker. HE was a rat.

ERIK

Where did you take him?

THE RAT WIFE

Down to the bottom of the sea, where the rats are. Everyone is the same there. No one has more. No one has less. Only peace. Por último.

ANDI

Finally.

THE RAT WIFE

Finally. …Okay. I'm feeling better. Gracias. Thank you. You're sure you don't need my help?

JOIE

We don't. Thank you.

THE RAT WIFE

Well, sweet one. You can never know for sure. If you change, or if anything comes gnawing at your feet, then you find me.

JOIE

Thank you. Goodbye.

> *THE RAT WIFE leaves. Time and space return as before.*
> *After a moment, JOIE covers her mouth and exits hurriedly.*

FREDDIE

Joie?

> *ERIK remains looking after THE RAT WIFE. Gradually over*
> *the following dialogue between FREDDIE and ANDI he slips*
> *away and is gone.*

FREDDIE (cont'd)

What was that?

ANDI

She didn't have nearly that much to say when I met her before.

FREDDIE

People actually hire that woman?

ANDI

SHE says so.

> *FREDDIE shakes his head and then looks at ANDI. THEY*
> *look at one another for a moment. THEY hug. The connection*
> *between them is warm.*

FREDDIE

How are YOU.

ANDI

I've spent a lot of time up here. You'll like it.

FREDDIE

And what about Dad?

ANDI

It's mostly settled. Just a few boxes of personal things I'm still going through. Old letters.

FREDDIE

Don't waste your time going through everything.

ANDI

I found some letters from my mother to him.

FREDDIE

That he saved? Old love letters?

ANDI

Not quite. If I'd known you were going to be here I might have brought them.

FREDDIE

I don't want to read your mother's love letters to our father. I'd rather not know about them.

ANDI

Freddie. She's my mother.

FREDDIE

Don't take it personally. It has nothing to do with you.

ANDI

What then? You need to forgive Dad. If he hadn't had an affair with my mother we wouldn't have each other. Think about that.

FREDDIE

I do. It's what it did to MY mother. The three of them are all together now. I'd hate to get caught under THAT cloud.

ANDI

Freddie when we have a chance, maybe after you've settled back in, we should talk.

FREDDIE

Of course.

ANDI

We have a lot to catch up on.

FREDDIE

Yes. But not your mother's love letters. I'm through with words, remember?

ANDI

…Freddie–

JOIE comes back in and sits down.

JOIE

–Ugh! I thought I was going to vomit. That woman smelled like rotten meat.

FREDDIE

She was pretty mesmerizing.

JOIE

Mesmerizing? You're head's still in Corsica.

FREDDIE

What she was saying about the bottom of the sea? I could imagine that's what it's like. I felt things like that many times these past several months. There's something undeniable about oceans and mountaintops when you really sit with them. Not like a tourist. But really spend time.

JOIE

I suppose you're going to want us to stay up here all the time now. What happened to you? I thought you were going for a tour of Europe, look at old buildings and drink espresso. You've always loved cities.

FREDDIE

I've changed. For the better I hope.

ANDI

So what exactly happened, will you tell us?

JOIE

I don't want to know.

FREDDIE

I have had a revolution inside.

JOIE

Oh my god.

FREDDIE

It must have already been in me when I suggested we build this place.

JOIE

This was going to be your writer's getaway. And now you've renounced writing.

FREDDIE

Now it will be something else. I did think a lot about you while I was gone.

JOIE

Uh huh.

FREDDIE

No. How grateful I am. Andi and I grew up with nothing. Just each other. And three warring parents who barely put food on the table, much less actual food.

JOIE

I've heard this story, come on.

FREDDIE

–But they were dreamers. I've come to appreciate that. Popcorn on Saturday nights and Dad would riff on all the incredible things

we'd do when our ship came in. Crazy out-there things. Like the
pirate ship hotel idea? And practical things. Good, normal things.
Like a dependable car. Or more than popcorn for dinner. Those
were dreams too. Between the drinking and the backstabbing
and the bitterness at having failed at everything they just couldn't
get it together to make any of them happen. Dad always blamed
capitalism but come on, he made choices. And thanks to you, Joie,
I've been able to make choices. That's what financial security is, let's
be frank: freedom of choice. One choice, as we know, was to devote
myself one hundred percent to writing a great novel about human
responsibility. I wouldn't have been able to do that without you.
And I wouldn't have had these past six months.

JOIE

Without ME? You WERE without me.

FREDDIE

Yes. And now I'm back.

JOIE

Without a novel to show for it.

FREDDIE

Right. Look. I left with no peace inside me. None. When Dad died
it hit me that now I'm really on my own. No one to blame. And I
didn't want to be like him. Or our moms. Always dreaming about
things and angry.

ANDI

But your novel wasn't a dream, it WAS something you were doing.

FREDDIE

No I was lost in it; chapters chasing chapters in circles. I spent
years proudly getting nowhere. "I was a writer!" Then, one night
in Umbria, a brilliant, clear sky kept me awake from dusk to dawn
with more stars than I'd seen on every night of my life put together.
I never felt tired once that night. And just when the sun rose. As if
to punctuate the dawn. A huge tree, fell, right next to me; it missed
me literally by inches!

ANDI

–Oh my god.

FREDDIE

–Something about that deep mesmerizing night sky, followed by
BAM: that tree, woke me up. I thought okay: the universe is putting
me in my place. That sky told me once and for all that I am small,
period. And then that tree, that ancient tree, used its last breath,
devoted its final act on earth to reminding ME, that life is short.
That I can't just go around enjoying the beauty of the world on my
wife's credit card and calling that the good life. Recognize beauty,
yes: and then live up to it! DO something! EARN the right to stop
and look at that sky. Of course I couldn't write the great thick novel
on human responsibility! Of course every sentence I wrote felt like
a desperate grasping in the air. I had no idea what I was writing
about! I've never been responsible in my life!

ANDI

–That's not true.

FREDDIE

–Not DEEPLY, no I haven't. Until I met Joie all I did was survive.
I couldn't afford to even think about doing more than that. I meet
Joie and boom: I can do whatever I want, which was such an exotic
concept for me I've been making up for lost time. No, I haven't been
Responsible. THAT's living. Thank you, Tree. And so here I am.

JOIE

And you're going to do what?

FREDDIE

Raise Erik.

JOIE

…What?

FREDDIE

Ever since the accident–

JOIE

–Freddie.

FREDDIE

–I've had a deep feeling in my heart that I've ignored.

JOIE

How much more can he be taken care of, Freddie.

FREDDIE

Infinitely more. I haven't been his father. Not fully. Not in my heart.
And after the accident–

JOIE

–Freddie.

FREDDIE

–After the accident, I made my novel my heart's first child.

JOIE

Oh god.

ANDI

Joie.

FREDDIE

No she's right it IS embarrassing. From now on, until he's a
man, I'm going to be His Father, and nothing else. I'll give him
everything my father didn't give me, and nothing that he did.

ANDI

Freddie.

FREDDIE

–The only good thing Dad gave us was dreaming. I'll give Erik that
and help him to make them actually happen.

JOIE

You're going to help him be a swimming rapper? Calm down,
Freddie.

ANDI

So you're never going to write your book? Later, when Erik's grown up. He said he wanted to read it.

FREDDIE

If he wants to read a great novel on human responsibility then HE can write it. Because he'll know what he's talking about. Because I'll have learned to teach him responsibility by finally taking complete responsibility for him.

JOIE

And when he's this Man, and on his way, then what will you do?

FREDDIE

I'll worry about that then. Right now I have to raise him.

JOIE

Freddie, you can do more than one thing at a time. Write your book, AND raise Erik, AND–

FREDDIE

–I'm going to be a father, Joie, and nothing else.

JOIE

Nothing else?

A silence. BERNIE arrives and breaks it with a knock-knock.

BERNIE

Hello. Is Everybody home? Looks like it.

ALL

Hello (*etc.*)

BERNIE

Home at last Freddie, I thought we'd lost you to Europe.

JOIE

His time was up.

FREDDIE

Everything must have its end.

BERNIE

Oh not everything I hope. Hello Andi.

ANDI

–Hi Bernie.

BERNIE

–I'm firmly convinced there are some things in the world that should never come to an end. Friends, a good house. Still standing is it?

FREDDIE

You must have done an excellent job designing it.

BERNIE

I think it's turned out quite well. I'm used to seeing Erik perched by the window, though, with his little eyes glued to his little screen. Where is he?

JOIE

He's somewhere.

FREDDIE

He might have slipped outside to play.

BERNIE

Does he still manage the landscaping? I made sure to keep the paths handicap accessible.

JOIE

He's barely "handicapped."

BERNIE

Oh I didn't mean–

FREDDIE

–We want him to get out more. Build his confidence.

BERNIE

Well it's good you have this place now to get away to. Such a beautiful area. I grew up in a woodsy area myself. I've always thought that having nature to play in as a kid made my imagination strong. But, the reason I stopped by, I was making one last check on the place, which I've grown so fond of, during our process together, and it's fortuitous I've found you all here to greet me so that I can tell you in person: that I have joined a new architectural firm, and my first assignment is taking me to [India].

ALL

Really? Oh! (*Etc.*)

ANDI

Permanently?

BERNIE

No. I'll keep my place in San Francisco. But it's quite an international firm, so I expect there will be many opportunities to travel. I've never been to [India].

FREDDIE

Congratulations.

BERNIE

Thank you. I really shouldn't be talking about it yet because technically my contract hasn't been signed. But that's just a matter of time. Hours, I hope.

JOIE

What are you waiting for?

BERNIE laughs but doesn't answer that, moving right on to:

BERNIE

Andi. Might you have time for one more tour of the grounds?

ANDI

Well, I just arrived myself and didn't actually expect to find everyone here. We were just catching up.

JOIE

It's okay Andi take a walk. It'll give Freddie and I a chance to wrap a few things up.

A silence.

BERNIE

Shall we? Just down to the river and back.

ANDI

All right.

FREDDIE

Could you check on Erik while you're out there?

ANDI

Sure. Okay. We'll be back.

BERNIE

See you both again shortly.

BERNIE and ANDI leave.

JOIE

He is all about her.

FREDDIE

Is he?

JOIE

Are you blind? And you know he was always stopping by when Andi would stay here.

FREDDIE

He's the architect.

JOIE

The place is finished.

FREDDIE

He's proud of his work.

JOIE

Do you not WANT to believe a man could be in love with your sister? Did you notice he didn't even mention the fact that he'd stopped by yesterday looking for her?

FREDDIE

Did he?

JOIE

When Erik was showing you the river. He popped in, just like this. Clearly he's been lying in wait.

FREDDIE

Does Andi like him?

JOIE

She said she thinks he's nice so I don't think so. Then again I can't say what's happened when they've been up here together. Andi did show up unannounced today herself, they could have had a rendezvous planned. And she's been very strange with me lately.

FREDDIE

How do you mean?

JOIE

Short answers. Doesn't look me in the eye.

FREDDIE

She's been dealing with Dad's death, his belongings, the paperwork.

JOIE

Maybe that's it. Or: maybe she's in love with the architect. And good for her. Sounds like he's doing quite well. She could get away to [India] instead of here.

FREDDIE

You'd prefer that.

JOIE

The poetry of HER breaking in the retreat we built for YOU wasn't lost on me.

FREDDIE

We didn't build this just for me.

JOIE

We didn't build it for Andi. And I didn't want it.

FREDDIE

You said yes.

JOIE

I always say yes, Freddie. Have you noticed? Yes, I'll have the baby. Yes, write your novel. Yes, build a cabin in the woods. Yes, go to Europe for fucking ever. Yes, I'll pay for it all.

FREDDIE

That's not fair.

JOIE

Fair? And then on some Italian mountaintop where you're supposed to be mourning your dead father and smashing writer's block, you instead have yet another revelation which has nothing to do with me.

FREDDIE

Erik has nothing to do with you, does he?

JOIE

Don't get moral. And don't act surprised, you know I never wanted a kid. But I had him. For you! Sometimes I hate you for it.

FREDDIE

Hate me!

JOIE

Yes, and everyone like you! Making me feel like a monster for
being a woman with ambitions other than motherhood. For
NOT wanting it all. For kicking ass at my job while you exercise
your whims. For wanting the sex that made me feel powerful
and vulnerable and capable of anything—like a complete human
being—to last and not get sucked from my body by children. When
we met we were the only thing you could think of. You remember
that?

FREDDIE

I do.

JOIE

I'd hate to think that was just one in your series of whims.

FREDDIE

–Joie.

JOIE

The first thing you should have done when I walked in that door
from work the other day was tear my dress off throw me on the
kitchen table and make my limbs quake. But you picked up Erik
and danced around the room with him like he was your bride to be.

FREDDIE

I hugged you and kissed you.

JOIE

That's right. Like your sister.

FREDDIE

What has happened to you?

JOIE

I've had six months to think, too, Freddie. At least your book wasn't
a living thing. This house is just wood and steel and glass. But I

can't take sharing you with Andi and Erik for the rest of my life. I married you. Not them. You married me. Not them.

FREDDIE

Erik is our son.

JOIE

He was a mistake. You know it. First for being conceived. And then that accident that may have made him our son forever. At least he's gay.

FREDDIE

What?

JOIE

Oh come on, he's clearly gay. And thank god. Gay people make a lot of money and now they play lead characters on TV shows. Unlike cripples who are (*pointing to her head*) "a bit slow." If he WASN'T gay he'd be more likely to end up dependent on us forever.

FREDDIE

You sound unbelievably hateful right now.

> *Throughout the following JOIE's tone is entirely sincere, compassionate, honest.*

JOIE

…The truth hurts. Don't think I don't feel it. But children are not the future. Old people are the future. Nobody gets younger. And there are more than the planet's share of people out there who WANT to have children. Who can think of nothing else BUT having children. Who work only and ever to afford CHILDREN. Let them. And God bless them. I'm not them. I love my job because what I'm doing is changing the world. And I love getting fucked by you because when I'm getting well and truly fucked by you my heart breaks over me and I forget about the world. And between changing the world and forgetting about it I feel entirely whole. Utterly satisfied. I DON'T need anything else. My body was made to have babies but my soul was never wired for motherhood. I never wanted to be one of those helicopter parents hovering over their child with all the paranoia of the Pentagon. All I want is to connect people virtually, and fuck you physically…

FREDDIE laughs uncertainly and shakes his head.

JOIE (*cont'd*)

It's baffling to you, I know. All my certainty. I seem hard to you. Because you're soft. You people without certainty, you people who don't know what you want or why you're here, always searching for the meaning of things and never finding it, you cannot fathom a perspective as simple and satisfying as mine. I'm hard. And you're soft. I'm definite. And you're diffused. You need me. And I need you. We're made for each other. We're one person. I don't want half of you. Or a third of you. I want Erik and Andi out of this house while I harden you and you soften me. That's how you and I work. That's how we met. That's how we'll always meet. And that's how we'll make it. And it's good. It's good. People die inside longing for what we have. You know I'm right. Say it. You know I'm right. Say it. Say it. Say you're right Jo. You're right Jo. You're right, Jo. You're right, Jo. Jo. ..Jo. …Jo. ….Freddie.

There is an intense energy humming palpably between JOIE and FREDDIE.

FREDDIE

You need to calm down.

JOIE

Do I sound worked up?

FREDDIE

You're frightening.

JOIE

Am I. …Do you remember what I was wearing when I came home and opened that door?

FREDDIE

A dress.

JOIE

Which one.

FREDDIE

The green one.

JOIE

The one you can never help peeling off me.

FREDDIE

But you didn't know I was going to be there.

JOIE

That's right. I wore it to work.

FREDDIE

Why?

JOIE

You can't possibly be the ONLY man who wants to peel that dress off me.

FREDDIE

…

JOIE

Don't think I wouldn't. Especially if you won't.

FREDDIE

You're threatening me.

JOIE

No I'm warning you.

FREDDIE

…That was the dress you wore the night of the accident.

If JOIE falters at all at this reminder, it's almost imperceptible.

FREDDIE (*cont'd*)

…You left Erik out on the table while I was peeling that dress off you.

JOIE

–Freddie?

FREDDIE

He fell on his head and broke his spine while I was peeling a green dress off you.

JOIE

Freddie.

FREDDIE

–That's what I remember about that dress.

JOIE

Erik's accident was not my fault. I wasn't alone when he fell.

FREDDIE

I asked you if he was all right and you said he was asleep.

JOIE

He was when I left him.

FREDDIE

On a table.

JOIE

And when we were done YOU fell asleep. The Sleep of the Just, was that it? While I went downstairs to check on him and found him lying there unconscious.

FREDDIE

If you hadn't left him–

JOIE

–If we hadn't HAD him! If we hadn't HAD him, Freddie!

ANDI bursts in hurriedly. She stands frozen, out of breath, looking at them. A silence before:

JOIE (*cont'd*)

…What is it, Andi? …I'm trying to get Freddie to fuck me, Andi, what is it?

ANDI

–Erik.

JOIE

…Erik what …Andi, come on! Erik what!

ANDI

Erik's drowned.

…After a stunned beat, an abrupt shift. THE RAT WIFE is standing in the river. Her flute beckons in the air. ERIK enters, standing on the shore, fixated on THE RAT WIFE. ERIK hobbles into the water with his crutch and wades deeper toward THE RAT WIFE, where he ends up floating on his back. THE RAT WIFE helps ERIK float along, gradually submerging with him, leaving his crutch or brace floating on the surface.

Scene Two

At the river. The next afternoon. FREDDIE is seated, staring at the water. ANDI arrives.

ANDI

I've been looking for you.

FREDDIE

…

ANDI

Have you been here the whole time?

FREDDIE

…

ANDI

You shouldn't just sit here, Freddie.

FREDDIE

They're not going to find him, I can feel it.

ANDI

…Freddie.

FREDDIE

–The air is still. Everything is so strange and still.

ANDI looks at everything and how still it is.

ANDI

It was that way in the city yesterday too. I came up here to get away from it. I had an odd feeling about it. And then when YOU were here I thought THAT must have been it but–

FREDDIE

…He's probably to the sea by now.

ANDI

Freddie.

FREDDIE

–Think about it. Twenty-eight hours? It's possible.

ANDI

Freddie stop.

FREDDIE

Can you even conceive the meaning of this?

ANDI

The meaning of it?

FREDDIE

There has to be a meaning. If I have to dig for it. I know Life Follows Nature but it can't all in the end be just a matter of fact. There has to be more to it.

ANDI

We'll never know what, Freddie.

FREDDIE

The whole thing is haphazard, a network of accidents, that's all life is.

ANDI

It WAS an accident. It doesn't have to mean more than that.

FREDDIE

If it doesn't mean–

ANDI

/ You're only going to torture yourself trying to dig an orderly meaning out of this, Freddie. Try not to make anything of it right now, give yourself time.

                                    FREDDIE

–How? I don't know what happened.

                                      ANDI

–You do know what happened.

                                    FREDDIE

–Those boys said they saw her standing in the middle of the river.
You can't stand in the middle of this river. An old woman who got
winded walking up a trail that was "made for the handicapped?"
They saw her go under with him. Where did she go?

                                      ANDI

She drowned.

                                    FREDDIE

Where are the bodies?

                                      ANDI

The police will find them.

                                    FREDDIE

She could have taken him somewhere.

                                      ANDI

The boys didn't see either of them come up. Freddie.

                                    FREDDIE

…I can't stop thinking about what she said.

                                      ANDI

You have to or you'll go insane.

                                    FREDDIE

I am. This is what it's like. I thought I knew what insanity was when
I couldn't think of what to WRITE. Now I know what it is. It's
nature's order.

                                      ANDI

…Have you talked to Joie today?

FREDDIE

I rather talk to you. Where is she?

ANDI

I left them sitting on the patio.

FREDDIE

Them?

ANDI

Bernie came by. He's with her.

FREDDIE

Bernie came by again.

ANDI

Mm-hmm.

FREDDIE

…He's a dependable man.

ANDI

He is.

FREDDIE

Do you like him?

ANDI

He's very nice.

FREDDIE

And?

ANDI

…He asked me– Yesterday. He asked me–

FREDDIE

…To marry him?

ANDI

No. He said, to make a promise. That he understands we've only known each other a short time. So, just a promise to get to know each other better. He had a promise ring. It was very sweet.

FREDDIE

And what did you say?

ANDI

I didn't. The boys started shouting from the river just then, an'–

A silence.

FREDDIE

…I remember when my mother died. And then when your mother died. We sat like this, up on Twin Peaks, looking over the city. It looked like a toy city from up there. Like we could rearrange it… You expect your PARENTS will die… And you made a joke about your mom's hair in the casket.

ANDI laughs.

FREDDIE (*cont'd*)

I've always felt most myself next to you. How long did you wear my clothes?

ANDI obviously knows what he's talking about, but:

ANDI

What? Your clothes?

FREDDIE

When I went away to college.

ANDI

(*Relents*) About a year.

FREDDIE

You used to wear them when we were little, too.

ANDI

I didn't have a choice then, we couldn't afford anything.

FREDDIE

What if you HAD been born a boy?

ANDI

Then people wouldn't have been confused that you called me Little Erik.

FREDDIE

It was your idea.

ANDI

My alter ego.

FREDDIE

Little Erik, wearing her big brother's old clothes.

ANDI

It was such a fun time in many ways. When you're a kid you don't know that you're poor until someone tells you. The street's a vast open playground and then someone tells you it's not safe.

FREDDIE

You were my little super hero.

ANDI

…Does Joie know I used to be called Little Erik? Did you ever tell her?

FREDDIE

I'm sure I told her. I can't remember but I must have.

ANDI

I hope not. If you did maybe that's why sh–

FREDDIE

...I forgot about him for a moment. We were talking about the past and he had nothing to do with it. How is it possible I could forget about him for even a second.

ANDI

You didn't forget about him. You were thinking about us when we were his age. That's all. You didn't forget about him.

FREDDIE

I'll never not think about him.

ANDI

Of course.

FREDDIE

I mean that I will never not think about him. Every waking moment I will look for him until I find him.

ANDI

Freddie sit down.

FREDDIE

I can borrow a boat from those people who live up the river.

ANDI

–Freddie.

FREDDIE

–They have a paddleboat tied to a dock.

ANDI

–Freddie you are not going to go looking for him. Sit down. Sit down. Facing me. ...Let's go up to the house. We can talk there. Or get some sleep. It's not a bad thing to not think about him for a moment. You need to rest from it.

FREDDIE

I can't imagine.

ANDI

You don't think of your mother every day. Or even Dad. I don't
either. It'll be a long time before we don't think of Erik for a day. But
even now it's okay if we let our thoughts go a bit, so it doesn't eat
away at us.

> *FREDDIE moves away. A silence. …FREDDIE turns back
> to ANDI and they look at each other intently. Their whole
> history can be felt in the ease and depth of it.*

FREDDIE

I'm so glad I have you.

ANDI

…You should go check on Joie.

FREDDIE

She's never been poor. Everyone in our family was poor. Makes you
see things a certain way. How things can change, (*snaps his fingers*)
right out from underneath you. We all share that. …JOIE can afford
to be sure of herself. …And we all have the same color eyes; except
you, "Little Erik black sheep."

ANDI

Freddie. Don't talk about that.

FREDDIE

Dad was never fair to you.

ANDI

Let's not talk about it.

FREDDIE

He should have been nicer to you. I told him so.

ANDI

I know. Thank you. Let's not talk about that now.

FREDDIE

He didn't love you like he should. And then toward the end when he got so much harder on your mother, and he would take it out on you, I wanted to make up for it to you. Like that summer when I was seventeen and you were fifteen.

ANDI

–It wasn't your responsibility. And my mother wasn't exactly–

FREDDIE

/ But, you're my sister.

> *Something in FREDDIE'S sarcastic delivery of that last line mocks a reprimand as to a teenager. He's referencing something.*

ANDI

Freddie? You should be thinking about Joie right now. She needs you. Her son's gone too.

FREDDIE

Oh, you have no idea.

ANDI

YOU have no idea.

FREDDIE

Me? What do I have no idea about.

ANDI

…Go up to the house, Freddie. And be with your wife. It's important. Okay? It's important.

> *JOIE and BERNIE arrive.*

JOIE

What's important?

A silence.

> BERNIE

Hello.

ANDI smiles to BERNIE.

> FREDDIE

How are you, Joie?

> JOIE

I came down to ask you the same thing.

> FREDDIE

I've been looking at the river.

> JOIE

All this time? Let's go back to the city.

> FREDDIE

I can't.

> JOIE

My phone's not working well up here. What if they try to call us.

> FREDDIE

They'll come find us. They know we're here.

> JOIE

At least come up to the house.

> FREDDIE

I'd like to stay here.

> JOIE

…Then I'll stay with you.

JOIE looks at ANDI. BERNIE notices.

BERNIE

Andi. I'll walk you back up if you like.

ANDI

Oh. Thank you.

ANDI looks at JOIE, then at FREDDIE, then to BERNIE for:

ANDI (*cont'd*)

Do you mind if we walk along the river a bit? There were some
flowers up the way I thought I'd pick some.

BERNIE

I'd be happy to go with you.

*BERNIE offers his hand. ANDI looks at it, takes it, looks at
their two hands, and they exit together. JOIE and FREDDIE
are silent for a moment...*

JOIE

Why didn't any of those boys try to save him.

FREDDIE

They're just boys.

JOIE

Andi says they're always by the river. They must know how to swim.
They made fun of him. They let him drown.

FREDDIE

...They gave you your wish then.

JOIE

...That is a horrible thing to say. Never for a moment have I wished
anything like this. That you didn't choose beTWEEN Erik and me,
that's what I wished.

FREDDIE

He's not between us anymore.

JOIE

No it sounds like he is, now more than ever. And you asked what happened to ME while you were away? You said I was hateful? While you've been sitting here staring at this river all day have you gotten up to look at your distorted face in it?

FREDDIE

You never loved him or wanted him. You admitted to it.

JOIE

I did love him Freddie.

FREDDIE

/ Half a day could pass and you wouldn't set eyes on him.

JOIE

I wasn't in a hurry. I thought we had a lifetime. And he never wanted me to love him.

FREDDIE

Never wanted you to! Because of me, I assume?

JOIE

Hardly. All you did for years was give him another book to read when you needed a break from failing at your own.

FREDDIE

–So why, then?

JOIE

–Andi! …Andi, he loved Andi. …After his accident, when she was taking care of him so often. That was my mistake. I avoided him. I felt horrible about the accident, Freddie. That wasn't my wish either. If I wished anything it was–

FREDDIE

…What?

JOIE

That Andi wasn't there, so that I couldn't have used her to avoid my part in what we did. Then maybe my son would have loved me as much as he did his Aunt Andi. And maybe my husband would have.

FREDDIE

Maybe.

JOIE

Don't be smug. You didn't love him either, admit it.

FREDDIE

I didn't love him?

JOIE

You said it yourself: your book—your great book about Human Responsibility! —THIS was your child. And when at last you realized you weren't actually equipped to raise it, you finally decided to be a REAL father—too late, as it turns out. Your grand epiphany to finally Embrace Fatherhood wasn't born of a deep untapped love for Erik! Erik was sloppy seconds when your book dumped you. And so you conCEDED to being a real father. But still not a real husband. That you yet cannot accept. Our son drowned yesterday and it's your sister you've spent today with, not your wife. Not your dead son's mother. You're not a father or a husband. You're a writer who never wrote.

> *FREDDIE doesn't object to what JOIE has said. He's listened to her. Maybe he even reaches out and connects with her physically. A silence. Then, not vindictive, but thoughtfully:*

FREDDIE

…Would you have given your life for his?

> *Likewise, JOIE's response is thoughtful, sincere and without malice:*

JOIE

No. I'd stay here, on earth. It's in life we might do something good.

JOIE checks her phone. No signal. She shakes it. Still no signal. She looks up at the sky.

FREDDIE

…What was it that journalist wrote about the Internet? The guy who wrote that article about you.

JOIE

That it's replacing memory. …It was an interesting question. How many generations will it be before memory is no longer a human trait, but a purely digital service.

FREDDIE

I can't imagine.

JOIE

It could be that it will feel no different. By that point we may have merged that much. Matter, energy, AND information—what the new physics people said a long time ago. They were right. They just didn't know information would get harnessed and made so readily tangible by an Internet.

FREDDIE

Memory robbed of its possibilities. The zeitgeist of its mystery.

JOIE

Can you really say you wouldn't erase certain memories if you could? Delete them forever?

FREDDIE chuckles ironically:

FREDDIE

They'll still have happened.

JOIE

Not if a search engine can't find them.

FREDDIE

It's not possible. Water will always find its way to the sea.

A silence.

JOIE

Maybe we should go on a trip together.

FREDDIE

You don't want to travel.

JOIE

Then let's throw open our doors and have parties and keep crowds of people around us. Something to pack our minds so we're not staring at this river all day for the rest of our lives.

FREDDIE

Maybe I should take up my writing again.

JOIE

Your writing! Yes, take it up again. Like a wall.

FREDDIE

–Between us, yes, exactly. What's bound us together until now is sex, money, and denial: the great trinity of our union. The only way to break it is to put a wall right through it.

JOIE

I love you, Freddie.

FREDDIE

You don't. And I don't love you. We have sex like molten lava that burns over everything in its path and that someday will burn itself out. Your money has been the exotic magic carpet I never thought I'd have the LUXURY to recline on. And denial has been the cooling salve for the burns of both. We don't love each other.

JOIE

Then why would you waste YEARS?

FREDDIE

–Because you're smart and rich and gorgeous and as willing to deny the truth as me. We ARE perfect for each other. It's terrible.

JOIE

How could you?

FREDDIE

That is a great question.

JOIE

What are you going to do?

FREDDIE

Teach.

JOIE

Oh yes, like Andi. Of course. You can teach together. You and Little Erik, together again.

FREDDIE

–So I DID tell you.

JOIE

Yes you told me. The night Erik JUNIOR had his accident. That's why we fought, remember? Because I was jealous and pissed and honest about it! And when we went upstairs to have make-up sex, Erik junior had a great fall. There's something unbelievably poetic about the whole thing, don't you think? Write about THAT, Freddie!

> *ANDI and BERNIE return. ANDI has some white flowers in her hand.*

JOIE *(cont'd)*

Hi Andi, we were just talking about you! Everything set with Bernie?

ANDI

What?

JOIE

Why don't we all head up to the house to celebrate! Freddie and I have managed to talk things through and we're good to go. Time for a party!

ANDI

What's going on?

FREDDIE

Yes, why don't you go on up and open a bottle of Champagne, Joie?

JOIE

Great idea. Bernie, mind escorting me to the house? I'm guessing the siblings have some family matters to finish up.

BERNIE

Oh. Okay.

BERNIE looks to ANDI questioningly.

ANDI

Go on Bernie. Thank you.

BERNIE

Thank you.

JOIE has left. BERNIE looks after her, then somewhat pleadingly to ANDI:

BERNIE (*cont'd*)

I'll see you soon?

ANDI

We'll follow you.

BERNIE exits quickly but apprehensively after JOIE. A wind is just now starting to blow. Over the course of the following it continues to pick up and with it the river grows gradually choppier.

ANDI (*cont'd*)

Freddie what is going on?

FREDDIE

I can't stand it here anymore.

ANDI

Then let's go up to the house.

FREDDIE

Here with Joie, I mean.

ANDI

What happened?

FREDDIE

Everything missing between us that's been gnawing at us for years, I think it's finally bit its way to the surface once and for all.

ANDI

What are you going to do?

FREDDIE

Leave here as soon as possible.

ANDI

Leave her?

FREDDIE

I said here, but her as well, yes! Can we just jump in your car and go, now?

ANDI

Freddie slow down.

FREDDIE

Let's get out of here and drive back home, you and me.

ANDI

Your home?

FREDDIE

Yours, I'll stay with you, it'll be like before.

ANDI

Freddie, wait.

FREDDIE

What is it? Bernie?

ANDI

No. It's not Bernie. You're in a panic right now. You're not thinking.

FREDDIE

I have never been more clearheaded. I've just been too weak to be clearheaded until now. Ever since that summer before I went off to college, when you were fifteen and I was seventeen, and we didn't know anything except that we felt safest with each other–

ANDI

/ Freddie, we're not fifteen anymore. You still love Joie.

With a broad dismissive gesture:

FREDDIE

I can get over whatever I might still love about Joie. I've never gotten over you. Never. You know it. You've known it all these years just like me.

ANDI

We can't go back in time, Freddie. It's too late. You owe Joie SOMEthing.

FREDDIE

I do. But it's an even trade. I wasted a good many of her best years as she did mine. I took advantage of her generosity and her money like a kid in a candy store who had never seen candy before in his life. But it's rotten! It's all rotten! What I was feeling in Greece and Corsica and Umbria before the immensity of sunsets and beneath the unfathomable vastness of night skies is what I've always felt with you. I get it now. I know it's wrong, but it's right!

ANDI

We can't, Freddie.

FREDDIE

We're brother and sister. It's a blood relationship that can't change.

ANDI

Maybe it CAN change. Maybe it has. Changed.

FREDDIE

How?

The moment of truth. ANDI knows it.

ANDI

...I told you yesterday that we should talk.

FREDDIE

Yes?

ANDI

...I told you I found some letters from my mother to Dad.

FREDDIE

Old love letters.

ANDI

Not love letters.

FREDDIE

What then?

ANDI

…You should read them.

FREDDIE

Why? …What do they say? …Andi? …What do they say?

ANDI

…They say– …Mom said– …Mom told Dad– …That I'm not his daughter. Someone else is my father. She lied to him. You and I are not brother and sister. …We're not brother and sister.

FREDDIE

We're not?

ANDI

We're not related. At All.

The look in ANDI'S eye is strangely elated. It feels like an explosion is about to happen between them. After a long moment, ANDI holds the flowers she'd picked out to FREDDIE.

FREDDIE

What are these?

ANDI

I picked them along the river. They were growing at the edge of the water. Take them.

FREDDIE

Why?

ANDI

–And then I'm going. Take them.

FREDDIE

Why.

ANDI

…One last gift from Little Erik.

The flowers tremble between them. THE RAT WIFE's flute can already be heard. FREDDIE whacks the flowers aside as they lurch toward each other and kiss, a deep passionate kiss that's been waiting for years to unleash itself. The wind is now chopping up the river fiercely as they sink to the ground. It's very clear that sex is going to happen and they're an exact match for each other. THE RAT WIFE plays her flute and crosses smoothly, waist deep, through the raging river.

Scene Three

At the house. That evening. (Over the course of the scene the sun will gradually set.) BERNIE is alone. He looks at the view. He checks his watch. He taps his feet lightly, distractedly, in odd patterns. Suddenly he busts out a dance. Now we know what those odd foot patterns were. He's surprisingly good. Like, "he should be on DWTS" good. ANDI enters with her bag(s) packed, seemingly on her way out. She stops when she sees BERNIE, who does not yet see her. His dance continues for a moment and she watches. On one of his spins he catches sight of her and is startled.

BERNIE

Ah! ...You're going then.

ANDI

You didn't have to wait for me.

BERNIE

I was enjoying the view. Everything is so still again after that wind. This has been a very strange summer. ...Well, despite the circumstances, I'm glad I was able to see you.

ANDI

Thank you, Bernie.

BERNIE

We can say our goodbyes here, unless you want to meet up again in the city.

ANDI

I need to go home.

BERNIE

Of course. Well. Goodbye then. But not for long I hope. And I hope, after some time, you might still consider my question.

ANDI

You're very persistent, Bernie.

BERNIE

An architect has to be. A house must stand the seasons.

ANDI

–Have you seen Freddie or Joie?

BERNIE

Yes.

ANDI

Together?

BERNIE

No. I'm not sure where they each are now.

ANDI

Have they seen each other do you know? Since I came back up to the house?

BERNIE

I don't.

ANDI

…Did you sign your contract?

BERNIE

Yesterday.

ANDI

When do you go to [India]?

BERNIE

Next month.

ANDI

(*to herself*) That long.

BERNIE

How long?

ANDI

Uh—yes, how long?

BERNIE

For a month, initially.

A silence.

BERNIE (*cont'd*)

I'm very sorry about little Erik.

ANDI looks up at him.

ANDI

What?

BERNIE

I said I'm very sorry about Erik.

ANDI

Yes, of course. Congratulations, again, on the new job. I'm sure it
will be great for you.

BERNIE

–Andi. I really do hope that you will consider my question. Maybe
before I go, or after I'm back, when this weekend is in the past, I can
ask it again. I wouldn't mind seeing [India] for the first time with
you. But I know that's very soon.

ANDI

I hear it's beautiful. I'm sure you'll be very happy.

BERNIE

Happiness is something between people. There's no happiness in
one person.

ANDI

I suppose there's something true to that.

BERNIE

Won't you try it?

ANDI

I did once.

BERNIE

You did.

ANDI

When I was fifteen.

BERNIE

Well. Didn't we all when we were fifteen. Where's that lucky boy now? Grown up like you and off living his life somewhere.

ANDI

He was my brother.

BERNIE

Oh. Well that's different. That's peace not happiness.

ANDI

What do you mean?

BERNIE

Family love is forever, it'll always be there in your blood. But that's not the feeling I meant. I meant a love between two people whose blood has nothing to do with each other. It's something else that connects them. Some spark in the dark marrow of our bones that no one ever sees. Not even us. We feel it. And when it flashes bright enough to reach up out of our bones and into our eyes, and we see someone else so clearly. That's happiness. When you can see yourself better because you've seen someone else so clearly. That's what I feel when I see you Andi.

ANDI

People change, Bernie.

BERNIE

Yes yes I can't worry about that. Build a strong beautiful home. Live inside of it. Travel the world outside of it. Come back to it—still standing, still functioning as it should, still warm when the world is cold and cool when the world sweats. The law of change is what it is. But it's not the only constant. I trust there are others.

ANDI laces her fingers into BERNIE'S with evident conflicted feeling.

ANDI

You are making this a lot harder than it needs to be.

BERNIE

I know.

ANDI

Why, Bernie?

BERNIE

I have to.

ANDI

Why?

BERNIE

Because I'm certain.

ANDI

How can you be so certain?

BERNIE

I can't explain it. It's not a house, nobody built it, nobody thought it through. It just is. And I trust it. I trust the weekends we've had in this house. I trust how I felt the mornings we woke up here together. I trust the way your leg draped over mine as you slept. I even trust that odd searching look in your eye when you stare at me. I'm certain.

ANDI

…You're lovely. I'm going to need more time.

BERNIE

…Should I call you?

ANDI

…I'll call you. That way you'll know for sure.

ANDI kisses BERNIE.

ANDI (*cont'd*)

Goodbye Bernie.

BERNIE starts to leave but runs into FREDDIE who is arriving.

FREDDIE

(*to ANDI)* Is Joie here?

BERNIE

No. Just Andi.

FREDDIE

Are you leaving?

BERNIE

I am.

FREDDIE

Alone?

BERNIE

I'm afraid so. For now.

BERNIE smiles clandestinely to ANDI.

FREDDIE

You have your things.

ANDI

Yes. I'm going too.

FREDDIE

With him?

ANDI

No.

FREDDIE

Stay here.

ANDI

No Freddie, I'm going home.

FREDDIE

I'll come with you.

ANDI

No Freddie.

FREDDIE

Stay here with me.

ANDI

YOU need to stay here, with Joie.

FREDDIE

I'm done with her. Unless you're staying here, I'm going with you, right now.

BERNIE

...Has something happened?

JOIE enters.

JOIE

Are you leaving?

ANDI

Yes.

FREDDIE

/ No.

JOIE

Uh. One more time. Are you leaving?

ANDI

Yes.

FREDDIE

/ No.

JOIE

I see. And you?

BERNIE

I was just leaving, yes.

JOIE

With her?

FREDDIE

No.

BERNIE

…No. For now.

JOIE

I see. And you? Where are you going?

FREDDIE

I don't know yet.

JOIE

Of course you don't.

ANDI

I'm gonna go.

FREDDIE

–Don't.

JOIE

–Yes, Andi, don't go. Stay here with us, I implore you. Take Erik's place for us.

ANDI

Erik?

JOIE

Yes. Isn't that what you'd like, Freddie? You used to call her your little Erik. Henceforth, Andi, you shall be our Erik.

ANDI

Freddie what have you said to her?

FREDDIE

Nothing. This is the first I'm seeing her.

JOIE

The first you're seeing me? Since what. Since what conversation that you two had.

ANDI and FREDDIE look at one another.

FREDDIE

…Andi?

JOIE

Say it.

ANDI looks at JOIE, then to FREDDIE.

ANDI

It was a mistake Freddie.

FREDDIE

A mistake? Andi–

BERNIE

–What has happened.

ANDI

It's been too long. It's not the right thing. You know it's not.

FREDDIE

What am I supposed to do? Stay with HER?!

And now ANDI'S tone shifts to one quite confident and aware.

ANDI

I wouldn't recommend it.

JOIE

Thank you Andi.

ANDI

Anymore than I would recommend you stay with him. Clearly it's not working.

JOIE

What did you two talk about!

ANDI looks at FREDDIE though she's answering JOIE:

ANDI

Old family business, that's all in the past. And now that it's settled we can move on.

FREDDIE

Andi.

                                    ANDI

–You go to [India] in a month?

                                   BERNIE

A little over three weeks.

                                    ANDI

And then back to San Francisco.

                                   BERNIE

Yes.

                                    ANDI

And then?

                                   BERNIE

Back and forth, depending on the projects I'm assigned, there or
elsewhere…?

                                    ANDI

/ Freddie, I'm going to leave my car here with you in case you need
to get yourself back to the city. I'll ride back with Bernie.

                                   FREDDIE

And then? You're not marrying him.

                                    ANDI

I've taken care of Dad's business. You need to take care of yours.
And no, I'm not marrying Bernie. But I'll write you when I get to
[India].

                                   FREDDIE

Andi!

        ANDI kisses FREDDIE. A solid, long, passionate, deeply felt
        final kiss goodbye. FREDDIE, BERNIE and JOIE are each
        stunned by this for their respective reasons.

ANDI

–Goodbye Freddie.

And ANDI exits abruptly. A brief silence before:

BERNIE

Enjoy the house.

BERNIE exits after ANDI. FREDDIE and JOIE are alone.
JOIE looks out, down to the river.

JOIE

There's a boat on the river. It doesn't look like the police. Whoever
it is probably has no idea how fucked up everything is. ...I suppose
you'll be hopping in Andi's car and chasing after her.

FREDDIE

No.

JOIE

Why when I was born did nobody consult me. Ask me if I
wanted to be a woman or a man. [Brown or white.] What kind of
personality, where to grow up. Nobody asks if you even want to be
born at all. Someone else makes this incredible decision for you.
No wonder we scream on arrival. It's the humiliation of being born.
Sometimes when I see pregnant women I want to punch them.

FREDDIE

Early on in my trip I was in Norway and I got lost hiking in a forest.
It got late. I panicked. I had no food, no flashlight. And I thought it
was entirely possible I might die. I figured if it were to happen then
I should fall asleep having made friends with Death. So I did. And
when the sun came up, I stood up and realized there was a little
town right down the other side of the ridge I was perched on. I'd
thought I was in the middle of nowhere. But I hadn't actually gotten
far from civilization At All.

JOIE

This really happened?

FREDDIE

It was embarrassing. I didn't mention it to you because I felt stupid. I'd thought I might die. What's more disturbing is how I'd made peace with it so quickly. What kind of life did I think I had, that dying was so acceptable? That I would go to sleep making friends with death? And now my friend has come and taken Erik.

JOIE

That's poetic.

FREDDIE shakes his head and smiles wearily.

FREDDIE

I hate you.

JOIE

…I guess in all honesty, my attraction to you has been, not logical. …What are we going to do?

FREDDIE

…I think Andi's right, Jo.

JOIE takes in a deep breath and lets it out.

JOIE

…Well then. Thank you Freddie, for these past ten years. You've carved out an empty space in me. And I must now fill it up. That gives me something to do.

FREDDIE

I'm sorry.

JOIE

I'M sorry. I bought you. (*a realization*) No. You sold yourself to me. That's it. And happily. I make bank, and you've been free to follow your whims. I've owned you. That's ALL. How did I not see it so clearly before?

FREDDIE

Because it's not something you can Google.

> *JOIE looks at FREDDIE. She goes to him and starts to beat the crap out of him with an incongruous coolness. The house starts to rattle. Likewise, the river below gets a bit choppy. JOIE and FREDDIE notice the house rattling and stop. The rattling grows a bit louder and the power flickers out just before the noise dies suddenly down and everything is still again.*

JOIE

I think that was an earthquake.

FREDDIE

A big one.

> *JOIE pulls out her phone.*

Who are you calling.

JOIE

–Oh good, full fan.

FREDDIE

Who are you calling?

JOIE

911.

FREDDIE

But we're fine.

JOIE

We have no power. There was an earthquake. It's an emergency. ... Oh! Busy.

FREDDIE

A lot of people are probably calling in. I don't see any lights from other houses.

> *A very, very distant siren can be heard, either a police or emergency alert siren.*

JOIE

I hear a siren. Do you hear a siren?

> *JOIE has dialed 911 again.*

FREDDIE

Joie don't keep calling. We're okay.

JOIE

We don't know that. …Still busy.

> *JOIE immediately dials again.*

FREDDIE

I saw some candles in the kitchen closet. I'll go look for them.

JOIE

…Oh! It's ringing. I got through.

FREDDIE

Let someone else get through. We're fine.

JOIE

Hello? Yes. There was an earthquake and our power is out. Can you send somebody?

FREDDIE

Joie…

JOIE

–Shh. What? …No, we're not hurt. But we're in the dark and our

house is way out in the woods above– …What? I'm sorry? …What?
…That's impossible.

FREDDIE

What is it?

JOIE

–Shh.

> *JOIE listens in shock and with complete attention to what the 911 operator is saying. Faintly in the distance what sounds like a church bell starts ringing, somewhat frantically.*

…So– What do we do? …Okay. …Okay. …Okay, we'll wait then. …
Okay. …Thank you, you too. Goodbye.

FREDDIE

What is it?

JOIE

That was an earthquake.

FREDDIE

I know. What happened?

JOIE

Downtown San Francisco collapsed. [San Francisco collapsed into
the Bay.][1]

FREDDIE

What?!

JOIE

She said if we're okay where we are, to sit tight and wait.

FREDDIE

For what!?

---

[1]The bracketed version of this line is the original. In performance it got a dramatically
unproductive laugh. The un-bracketed version was instated mid-run and did not elicit the
laugh. This might not be an issue outside the San Francisco Bay Area. Productions are
free to use the line that works best.

JOIE and FREDDIE notice the eyes of a thousand rats glowing in the cracks of the house and the surrounding woods. The flute of THE RAT WIFE cries out abruptly and then continues to play. THE RAT WIFE walks into the house. JOIE and FREDDIE look at her. She walks past them and out another door. All the rats follow her. JOIE and FREDDIE are alone again.

The end.

Afterword

Reviewers were wide-ranging in their responses to *Little Erik* during its Aurora Theatre Company premiere, with some quite enthusiastic, some split down the middle and others almost comically damning. Though some embraced the moral and emotional complexity of the characters and situations, complaints followed the basic trends that greeted Ibsen's original—namely, moral judgments leveled against how characters handle their grief and their tangled relationships, as well as objections to the play's mix of styles and its ending. (My ending and Ibsen's differ radically yet share a certain suddenness of turn.)

There was something at once comforting and troubling about this century-spanning consistency. Comforting in that, if mixed reviews are good enough for Ibsen they're good enough for me. Troubling because it would seem aesthetic and substantive expectations in theatre might not have advanced substantially since 1895! Despite life's undeniable messiness, we often don't allow our theatre to reflect this, preferring it support our ideals instead with neat narratives, tidy praise for good behavior and swift justice against characters who embarrass us with their frankness or failings.

I did not set out to fix Ibsen's play. It misbehaves in ways I find exciting and productively problematic. (The title itself, which seems to reference the child, Erik, while actually pointing to Andi, plays with our expectations of consistent dramatic structures built around single protagonists.) I wrote *Little Erik* to encourage compassion for people going through great personal trauma, trying their best and failing. Who are we to judge another person's grief? Or how they handle their troubled relationships? Don't we hope our friends and neighbors will grant us their understanding when we inevitably stumble through life's tangles?

I was gratified by how often audience members at the Aurora approached me and the cast to express their appreciation for the play's brutal honesty about grief and gender roles. While

Little Erik provides too few answers for some, it excites others to ask more questions of themselves. For some people it offers an ugly, repulsive clutch of caricatures, while others find in it a compelling group of recognizable, flawed human beings. In this and other ways, the play embodies the human struggles it aims to depict. This is Ibsen's genius and I am pleased if I did not improve upon his accomplishment.

Mark Jackson
February 2017

About The Author

Mark Jackson is a playwright, director and performer. He was the founding artistic director of Art Street Theatre, San Francisco, from 1995 to 2004, during which time he wrote, directed and performed in numerous productions for the company. Mark's range of work in theatre, dance and performance has been seen in the San Francisco Bay Area at Aurora Theatre Company, Encore Theatre Company, EXIT Theatre, Marin Theatre Company, Potrzebie Dance Project, San Francisco International Arts Festival, The Shotgun Players and Z Space. Nationally at The Catamounts (Denver), Hunger & Thirst (NYC) and The Studio Theatre (Washington D.C.). Internationally at Arts International Festival IV (Japan), Edinburgh Festival Fringe (UK), Bread & Roses Theatre (UK), and Deutsches Theater Berlin (Germany). His plays have been developed at American Conservatory Theater, Capital Stage, Cutting Ball Theatre, EXIT Theatre, Magic Theatre, Playwrights Foundation and Z Space.

Mark has been a resident playwright at English Theatre Berlin (Germany) and the Djerassi Resident Artists Program, where he was awarded the William and Flora Hewlett Foundation Honorary Fellowship. He is a German Chancellor Fellow of the Alexander von Humboldt Foundation, which has supported Mark on three extended artist residencies in Berlin. Other awards and honors include the Edgerton Foundation New American Plays Award, a Magic Theatre / Z Space New Works Initiative commission, a Bridging the Gap grant, and the San Francisco Bay Guardian Goldie Award. Mark's writing has benefited numerous times from the generosity of the Tournesol Project, a granting program for the development of new work. He has been a company member of The Shotgun Players since 2010.

EXIT Press published *TEN PLAYS*, the first collection of Mark's work, in 2010, and a second collection, *THREE PLAYS*, in 2012.

MORE PLAYS FROM EXIT PRESS

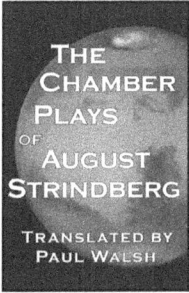

THE CHAMBER PLAYS OF AUGUST STRINDBERG: TRANSLATED BY PAUL WALSH

New translations by Yale drama professor Paul Walsh of the intimate chamber plays of August Strindberg, one of the major pioneers of naturalism in the theater: *The Ghost Sonata, Storm, Burned House, The Pelican, and The Black Glove.*

THREE PLAYS BY MARK JACKSON

"Playwright/director Mark Jackson has made his name as a first-class theatrical provocateur. Gutsy showmanship, brainy literary instincts and laser-sharp satire mark his canon." — San Jose Mercury News
The second collection of plays by Mark Jackson includes three plays based on incredible historic events: *God's Plot*, *Mary Stuart*, and *Salomania*.

SONGS OF HESTIA: PLAYS FROM THE 2010 SAN FRANCISCO OLYMPIANS FESTIVAL

Playwrights Nirmala Nataraj, Bennett Fisher, Stuart Eugene Bousel, Claire Rice, and Evelyn Jean Pine adapt some of Western culture's oldest stories, illuminating our present-day concerns with imagination, creativity, curiosity and passion.

HILARITY BY ALLISON PAGE

A play about a girl named Cyd. She's not so nice. She's not so sober. She's not so happy. But she is funny. Cyd is a comic on the edge of destruction. Liz is the only person keeping her from pickling herself to death. Maybe she'll turn it all around, or maybe her drunken lies, hungover manipulations and impulsive violence will finally bury her. Does it matter if you're good at something, if you don't know how to be a person?

EXIT Press is the publishing division of EXIT Theatre, a San Francisco theater company founded in 1983.   www.exitpress.org

www.ingramcontent.com/pod-product-compliance
Lightning Source LLC
LaVergne TN
LVHW011408080426
835511LV00005B/436